A-Star Question Bank

A-Star Question Bank

James F. Frayne

MONTANA PUBLISHERS

First Printing: 2016

ISBN 978-1-326-60677-0

(Also available 'With Solutions': ISBN 978-1-326-65018-6)

Montana Publishers

Front Cover: *Inspired by the beautiful open star cluster of Pleiades, otherwise known as the Seven Sisters or Messier 45.*

Design of internal first page: Hayley Jane Smith.
Inspired by the fresco "School of Athens" painted by Raphael between 1509 and 1510, this portion depicting Plato and Aristotle.

Information:
Special discounts are available on quantity purchases by corporations, associations, educators, and others.
For details, contact the publisher at the e-mail address detailed below.

U.S. trade bookstores and wholesalers please contact publishers at:
e-mail: EAYG2014@hotmail.com

Normal purchases can be made at: www.Lulu.com
(Delivery generally within two to three working days).

By the same author:

Easy as you Go! A Mathematical Companion (Volume 1: A – L)

Easy as you Go! A Mathematical Companion (Volume 2: M- Z)

A-Star Mathematics Question Bank (With Solutions)

Selected Biology Advance Level Topics Volume 1 (A to J)

Selected Biology Advance Level Topics Volume 1 (K to Z))

Tall Grows the Grass (Full Novel)

Tall Grows the Grass (Books 1 – 3)

Hell Bank Notes (Catalogue of Contemporary Issues)

Romancing the Wood (Wooden Nickel 'Flats' of the USA)

The Indian Hundi (A Collection of Indian Scrip)

For more details, please visit author's website at http://jamesfrayne.net

Contents

PROBLEMS (SOLUTIONS)

Contents

PROBLEMS (SOLUTIONS)

Contents

PROBLEMS (SOLUTIONS)

Contents

PROBLEMS (SOLUTIONS)

Contents

PROBLEMS (SOLUTIONS)

Contents

SOLUTIONS (PROBLEMS)

Contents

SOLUTIONS (PROBLEMS)

Contents

SOLUTIONS (PROBLEMS)

Contents

SOLUTIONS (PROBLEMS)

Contents

SOLUTIONS (PROBLEMS)

Preface

The general yard-stick for 'attention span' is 2 to 5 times a student's age. That means that, on the average, the level of attention tails off quite dramatically as one heads towards the end of one hour.

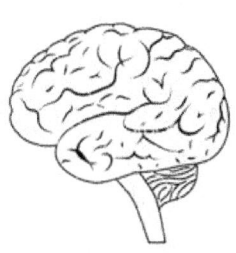

Admittedly, this is only a 'rule of thumb' but it based on a number of important premises. Not least of all is the fact that the brain is the organ that consumes more oxygen than any other one in the body.

This is about 20% of the total oxygen used by our body over the same time. In the brain the rate of consumption of oxygen does not generally change in percentage nor in amount - in other words, it is constant - per gram, per minute. But this does not discount the fact that if there is just not enough oxygen entering the body then the brain will undoubtedly suffer. When the brain does not get the necessary supply of oxygen it can become 'hypoxic' and this can lead to poor concentration, forgetfulness, and low drive.

Generally, if you are slouched over an examination paper in a bad position, you are not receiving your normal supply of oxygen, so this can only have a detrimental effect with regard to oxygen supply to the brain.

It is not surprising, therefore that concentration wanes as a student wades through their examination paper. To make matters worse, the examination paper is normally constructed to help candidates fail

Preface

The papers usually have easy questions at the beginning, followed by the high mark, more difficult questions towards the end of the paper (precisely when students are getting worn out, suffering from a tail-off of their general attention, and with their brains not working at full capacity through a depleted supply of oxygen). In other words an inbuilt recipe for disaster!

It is not that the end paper A and A* questions are that much more difficult, only that they usually combine more than one mathematical principle. They therefore require that much more concentration.

If that was all, then with practice most students could be well able to identify the salient parts to a posed problem, but there is all too often another animal lurking in the wings and that is the ubiquitous 'Drawings not to Scale'.

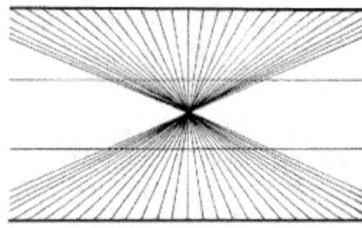 Take a look at the drawing on the left. Are the horizontal line in the middle parallel or not? Most of us would say 'Yes, they are parallel', but there is a large caucus of us who would insist that they are not!

That is straightforward enough, but now try the next one!

Preface

This geometrical drawing is perhaps not too unfamiliar in style to many that all of us have got used to in our study of Mathematics, and the question is rather a simple one: 'In the drawing below, which is the longer line, AB or BC?'

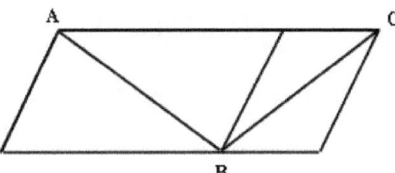

Of course, the answer is obvious; it is line AB. There is no sense in confusing the issue and the drawing is presented to the student and the question is simply put. If you decided on line AB, you would be wrong – the answer is that both lines are the same length. It is all a matter of perception and unfortunately the examiners are Mathematicians and not Psychologists.

All too often a question is accompanied by a drawing which slaps in the face of psychological perception idiosyncrasies.

This is true of many drawings whether straightforward 2D drawings including line, circles or both, but is more perplexing when the problem involves 3D drawings.

Preface

Concentrate for one minute on this 3D figure and see what happens.

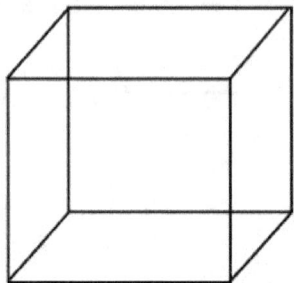

This is a very simply drawing of a cuboid It is called a Necker Cube.
– any cuboid would be the same. Yet the effects can be confounding,
confusing and even disturbing. It is not surprising that, faced with a
3D drawing of a cuboid in the examination, most students are often
bewildered and suffer the same effect as you probably experienced on
concentrating on the above figure.

So what do we do about this? What do we do to address the problem
of a waning concentration, and difficulty in tackling figures which
are, in all good faith, placed there in the question to help the student?

We can encourage the student, the prospective examination
candidate, to familiarise themselves with the variety of questions that
they may come across in their Mathematics examination paper.

Preface

You may say 'But this is exactly what is being done in our schools right now with students going home with a bunch of past papers to work through'.

Yes, this is fine stuff, but answer the question 'How often are the wrong answers corrected and if so are the solutions, particularly to A and A* questions, corrected to the complete and utter satisfaction and understanding of the student?'

If the answer is resoundingly positive, then in all probability students, maybe your son or daughter, do not need this book. Otherwise, the worked answers will speak for themselves. Familiarity with the various figures employed in questions, together with the questions themselves, will be a great asset and add to the armoury of resources that are at their disposal.

In any event, the 100+ mathematical problems posed in this book will certainly titivate the interest of the compulsive puzzle aficionados among us!

James F. Frayne
June, 2016

Problems

Problem 01 Solution 69

In triangle ABC, D is a point on BC.

Calculate the angle x.

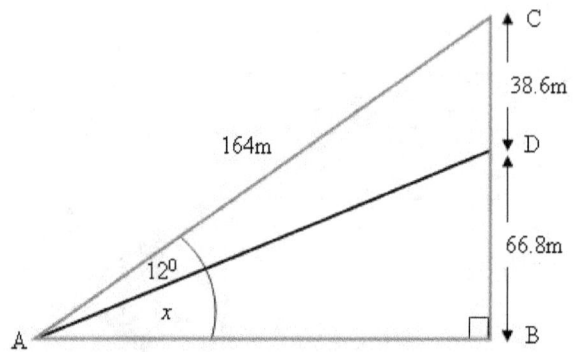

Problem 02 Solution 77

A child's toy is made by joining a cone to a hemisphere.
The hemisphere and cone each have a radius of 5cm.
The slant height of the cone is 12cm.

a) Show that the total height H of the toy is 15.9cm.
b) Calculate the total volume of the toy.

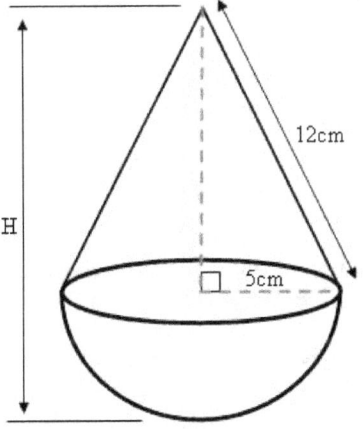

Problem 03 Solution 37

Solar cells are often included in modern building designs. The
symmetrical design for a solar cell is shown below.

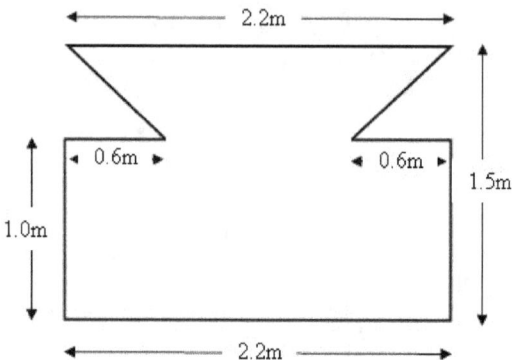

When tested, the solar cell is shown to have a maximum power of
860 watts from an input of light of 950 watts/m².

Show that the area of the solar cells is 3m², and use this to
calculate its energy conversion efficiency.

Problem 04 Solution 13

Here is the graph of $y = \sin x$ for $0^0 \le x \le 360^0$

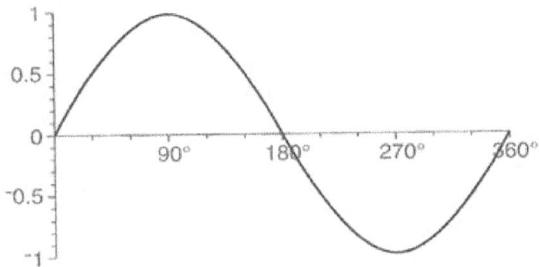

Calculate the two solutions of the equation $\sin x = 0.2$ for the values of x between 0^0 and 360^0

Problem 5 Solution 62

In the quadrilateral below:

- angle b is twice the size of angle a
- angle c is 40^0 more than angle b
- angle d is half the size of angle c.

Work out the size of the largest angle in the quadrilateral.

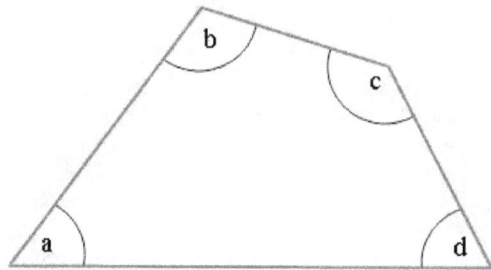

Problem 06 Solution 97

ABCDE is a regular pentagon.
ACFG is a square.

Work out the size of the angle DCF.

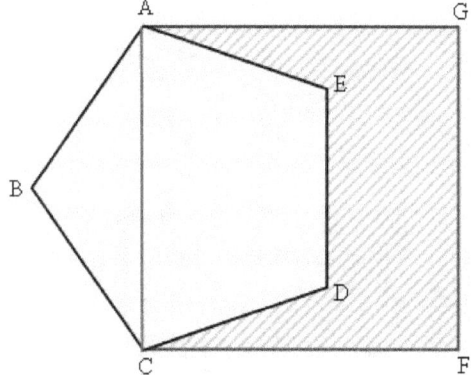

Problem 07 Solution 48

In the diagram, A and B are points on the circumference of a circle, centre O.
PA and PB are tangents to the circle.

Calculate angle b.

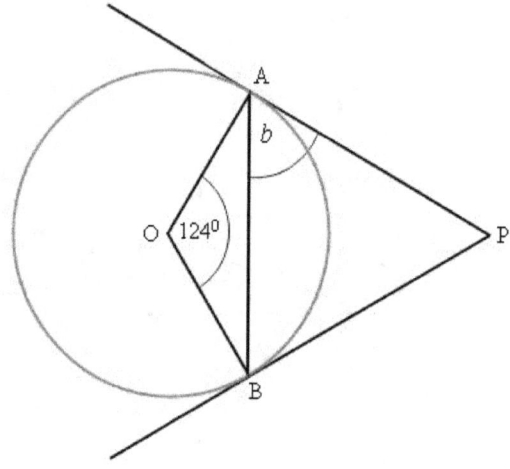

Problem 08 Solution 67

a) A hi-fi speaker is a cuboid measuring 15cm by 20cm by 30cm. Two of these speakers are packed into a box with internal measurements 40cm by 25cm by 40cm.

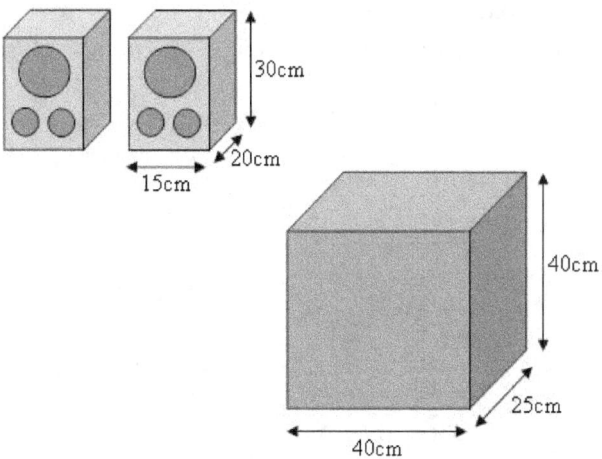

The rest of the space inside the box is filled with polystyrene. Calculate the volume of polystyrene.

b) An amplifier is packed into a box measuring 20cm by 15cm by 10cm.
Calculate the surface area of the box.

Problem 09 Solution 85

P, Q and R are points on the circle, centre O.
TA and TB are tangents to the circle at P and Q.
Angle PTQ = x

a) Show that the angle TPQ = $90^0 - \tfrac{1}{2}x$
    Give reasons for each step.

b) Prove the Alternate Segment Theorem by showing that angle
    PRQ = angle TPQ
    Give reasons for each of your statements.

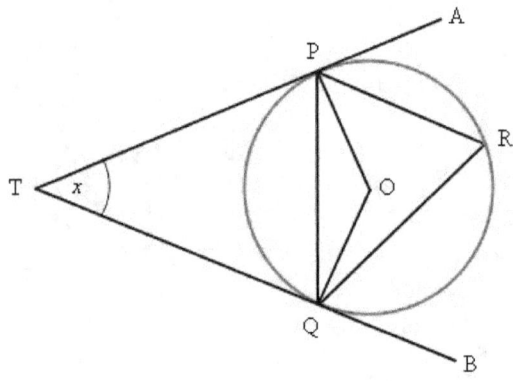

Problem 10 Solution 30

In triangle XYZ, S is a point on XZ such that $\overrightarrow{XS} = 3\ \overrightarrow{SZ}$, and T is a point on ZY such that $\overrightarrow{YT}$ is 3 $\overrightarrow{TZ}$.

Prove that $\overrightarrow{ST}$ is parallel to $\overrightarrow{XY}$, and ¼ the length of $\overrightarrow{XY}$.

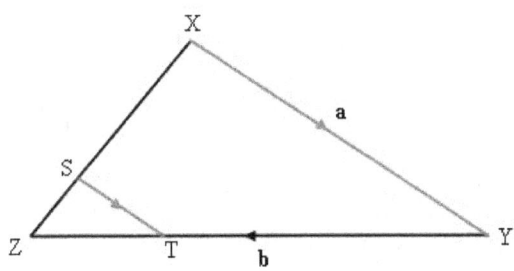

Problem 11 Solution 18

A cuboid, ABCDEFGH, has 2cm, 3cm and 4cm.
Calculate the length of diagonal AG.

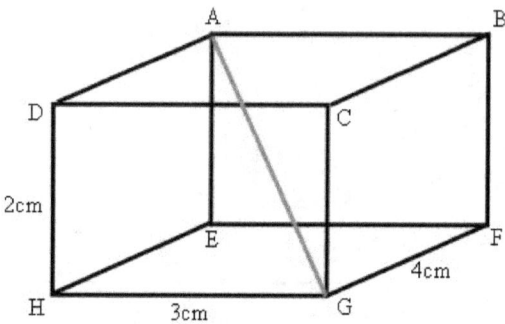

Problem 12 Solution 53

Max stands at a point A on the bank of a river with parallel straight sides.

He sees two posts at B and C on the other side of the river. He knows that the posts are 100 metres apart.

The angle between the bank and the line AB is 30^0.
The angle between the bank and the line AC is 35^0.

Work out the width of the river w.

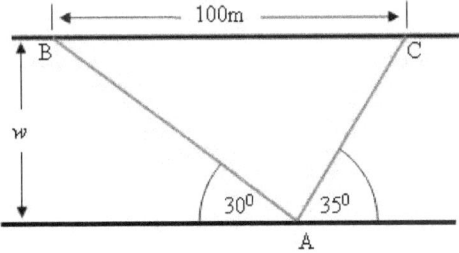

Problem 13 Solution 70

Here is a rectangle:

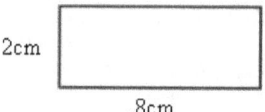

2cm

8cm

The eight-sided shape is made from four rectangles and four congruent right-angled triangles.

Work out the perimeter of the eight-sided shape.

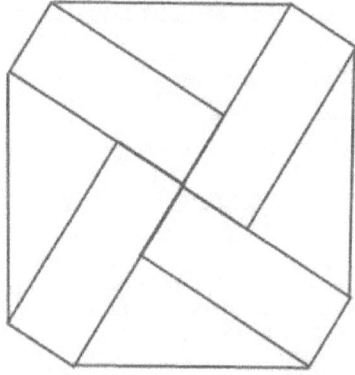

Problem 14 Solution 66

The square shown below has sides measuring 4x

M is midpoint of side CD

Point N cuts the side AD in the ratio AN : ND ~ 3:1

a) Find the sizes of BN, NM and BM

b) Prove that angle BMN is a right-angle

c) Hence find the area of triangle BMN

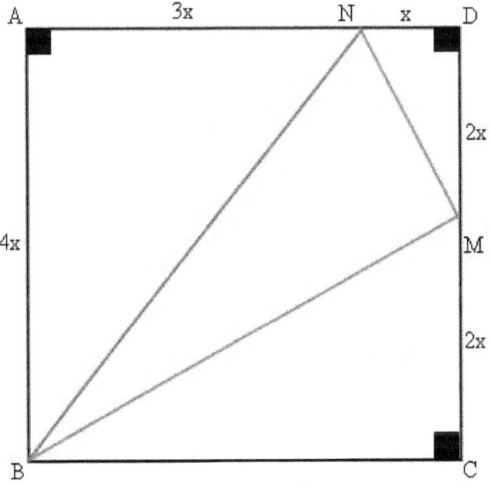

Problem 15 Solution 45

Given then points A(-1,1), B(1,-2) and C(2,3),

a) Find the vectors $\vec{AB}$, $\vec{AC}$, $\vec{BC}$

b) Find the magnitude of each of the vectors in part a)

c) Hence prove that ABC is a right-angled triangle.

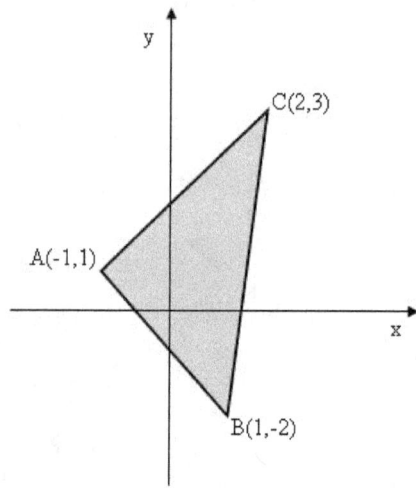

Problem 16 Solution 04

This method of navigation was used before the Global Positioning System (GPS) was introduced.
It is called 'doubling the angle at the bow' and was used to calculate the distance between a ship and a point on land (eg: a tower).
A ship is travelling along the straight line AB.
A tower is at C.
When the ship is at A, the bearing of the tower at C is x,
The ship continues to B where the bearing of the tower is 2x.

Show that the distance BC is equal to the distance that has been travelled by the ship from A to B.

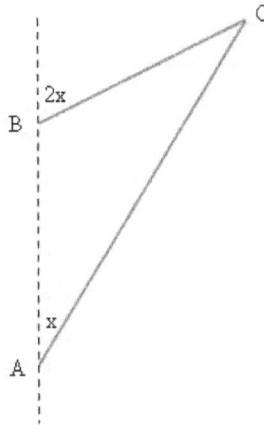

Problem 17 Solution 02

ABCD and PQRS are mathematically similar.

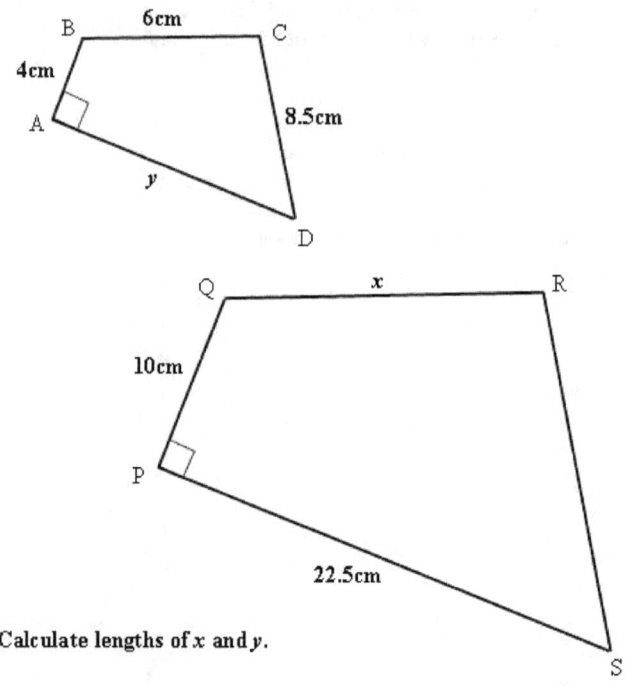

Calculate lengths of x and y.

Problem 18 Solution 107

A rectangle has a semicircle of radius 6cm removed.

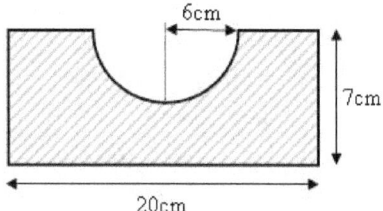

Find an expression, in terms of π, for the shaded area.
Give your answer in the form $a - b\pi$.

Problem 19 Solution 26

Here is a sketch of a logo.
The diamonds have two lines of symmetry and the interior angle
at its base is 85⁰.

Calculate the angle labelled y.

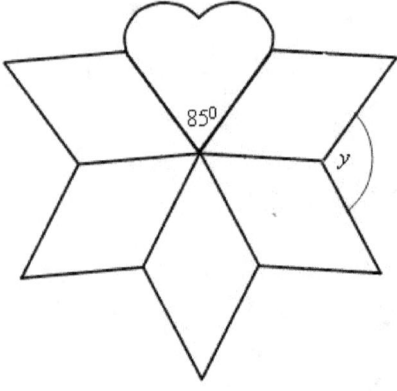

Problem 20 Solution 104

This is a diagram of a field where Lucy wants to keep horses.
Each horse must have one acre of field.
One acre is equivalent to 4046 m².

What is the largest number of horses Lucy can keep in this field?

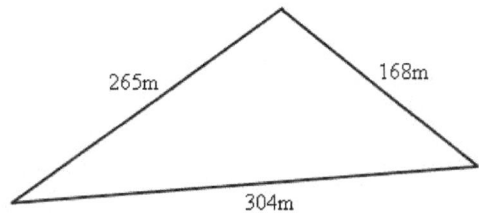

265m

168m

304m

Problem 21 Solution 68

To steer a course midway between two rocks, P and Q, a ship
needs to ensure that the bearings of the two rocks are x and
$(360^0\text{-}x)$ respectively.

A ship at C is equidistant from P and from Q.
Show that PD = QD.

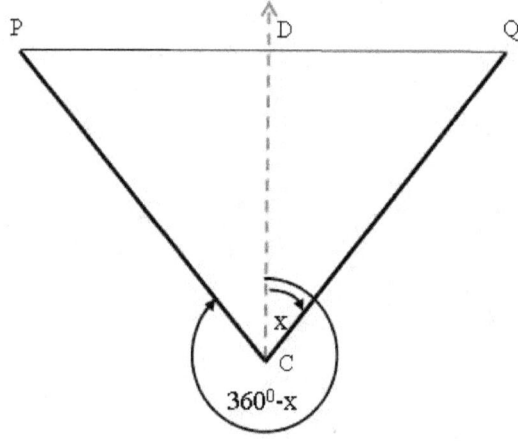

Problem 22 Solution 100

ABCD is a square.
P and D are points on the y-axis.
A is a point on the x-axis
PAB is a straight line.
The equation of the line that passes through the points A and D is
y = -2x+6.
Find the length of PD.

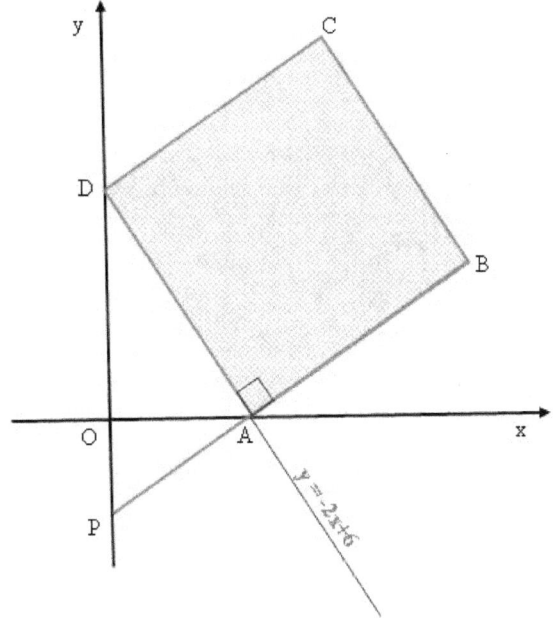

Problem 23 Solution 72

ABCD is a quadrilateral.
BA is parallel to CDE.
Angle h is <u>not</u> equal to 126^0.

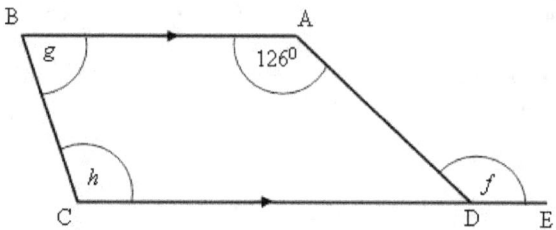

a) What is the mathematical name for quadrilateral ABCD?
b) Find the size of angle f giving your reason for your answer.
c) Angle h is 4 times the size of angle g.
    Work out the size of angle h.

Problem 24 Solution 96

In the diagrams below, the perimeter of the square is equal to the perimeter of the rectangle.

Show algebraically that the area of the square is greater than the area of the rectangle.

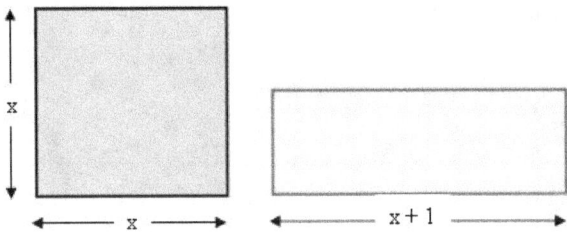

Problem 25 Solution 51

The diagram shows a classroom in the shape of a cuboid.
O is the origin, A is (8, 0, 0), B is (0, 7, 0) and C is (0, 0, 3).

a) What are the coordinates of D and E.
b) A light is to be fitted at the midpoint of the ceiling edge CF.
   What are the coordinates of this point.
c) A projector is to be fitted at the centre of the ceiling.
   What are the coordinates of this point.

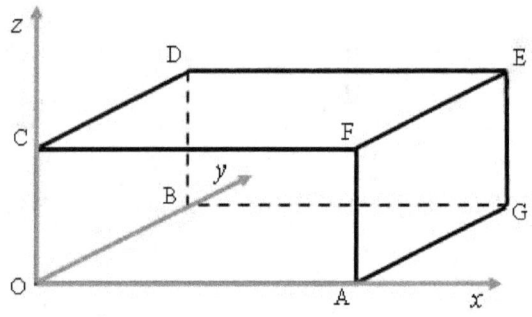

Problem 26 Solution 64

a) In the diagram below, AB is parallel to CD.

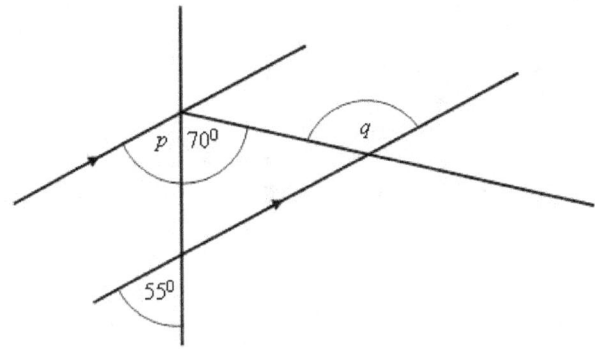

Work out angle *p* and angle *q*, giving reasons for your answer.

b) The exterior angle of a regular polygon is 40^0.
How many sides does the polygon have?

Problem 27 Solution 106

At 'The Oval Theatre' there are three different prices, adult, child and student.
Henri finds three receipts for tickets for the same performance.

Work out the price for an adult, student and child.

The Oval Theatre	The Oval Theatre	The Oval Theatre
5 Adults	2 Adults	4 Adults
3 Children	1 Child	2 Children
	3 Students	
Total: £85	Total: £58	Total: £65

Problem 28 Solution 63

A company makes bronze statues in two sizes.
The small statue has a surface area of 320 cm² and a volume of 420 cm³.
The larger statue is mathematically similar and has a surface area of 720 cm².

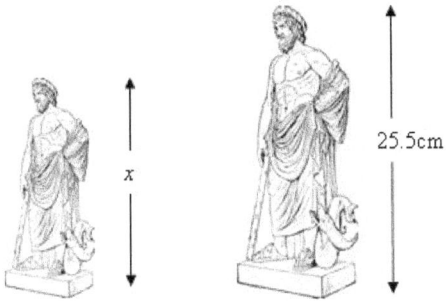

25.5cm

x

a) The volume of the large statue is given by this calculation:

$$\text{Volume} = 420 \times \left(\frac{720}{320}\right)^{\frac{3}{2}}$$

Work out the volume of the large statue.
Give your answer correct to three significant figures.

b) The height of the large statue is 25.5cm.
Calculate the height x of the small statue.

Problem 29 Solution 82

A tent is in the shape of a pyramid with a horizontal rectangular base ABCD.
The vertex E is directly above the centre of the base X.
The height of the pyramid is 7m.

Work out the size of the angle that EB makes with ABCD.

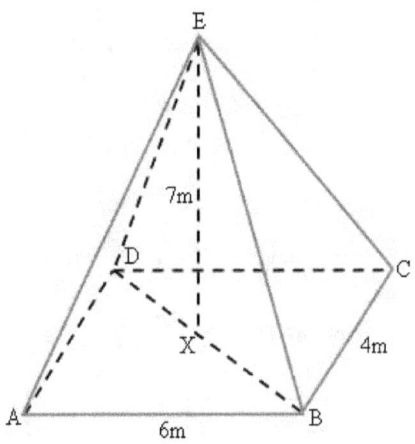

Problem 30 Solution 61

The vertices of the triangle ABC lie on the circumference of a circle.
DA and DC are tangents to the circle.

Work out angles x and y giving reasons for your answers.

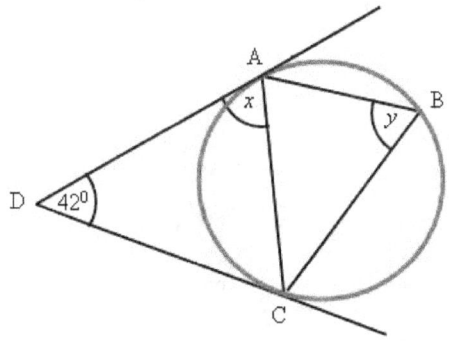

Problem 31 Solution 42

a) Show clearly that the surface area, S, of a cylinder of radius r
    and thickness t is given by:

$$S = 2\pi r \, (r + t)$$

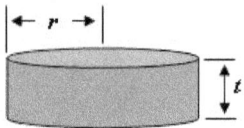

b) Red blood cells are roughly cylindrical in shape.
    The cells absorb oxygen on their surface.
    This is then carried round the body.
    When red cells stick together, there are fewer faces to absorb
    oxygen.
    They stick together like coins in a pile.

    Find and simplify an expression for the difference in area in the
    surface area of n free cells compared with n cells stuck
    together.

Problem 32 Solution 80

The diagram shows a container the shape of a cone.
The radius of the top is 8cm and the vertical height is 24cm.
Both of these measurements are correct to the nearest centimetre.

Calculate the upper bound for the volume of this cone.

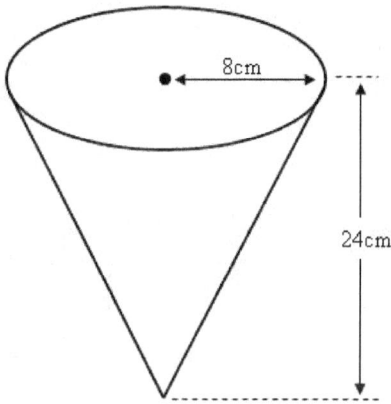

8cm

24cm

Problem 33 Solution 28

A gate is made from strips of metal.
The outline of the gate is a rectangle topped by a semicircle.

a) Explain why the maximum height of the gate is 190cm.

b) Work out the total length of metal strip needed to make the gate.

c) Give your answer correct to three significant figures.

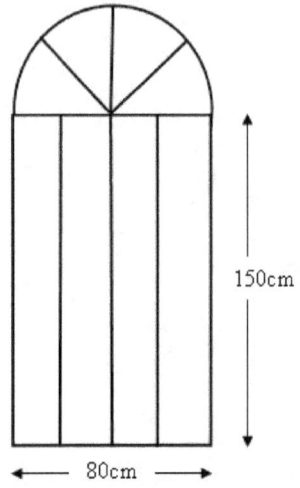

150cm

← 80cm →

Problem 34 Solution 21

Benny buys a new washing machine.
In the first year the probability that this machine has a fault is 1/20.
In the second year the probability that it has a fault is:

• 1/5 if it had a fault in the first year
• 1/10 if it did not have a fault in the first year.

a) Complete the tree diagram to show these events.
b) Work out the probability of this machine having <u>at least</u> one fault in the first two years.

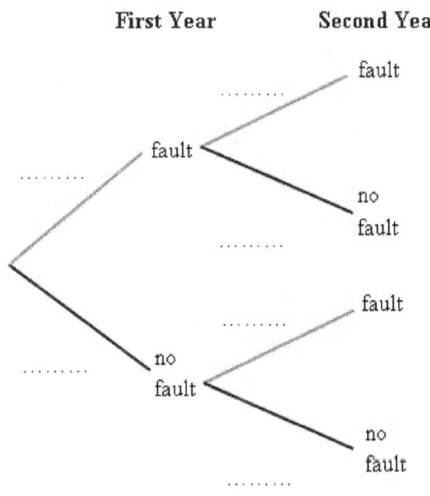

Problem 35 Solution 16

This diagram shows parallelogram ABCE.
D is a point on EC.
AD = BD, angle ADE = 70⁰ and angle CBD = 10⁰.

Work out angle BCD.
Give reasons for each angle you work out.

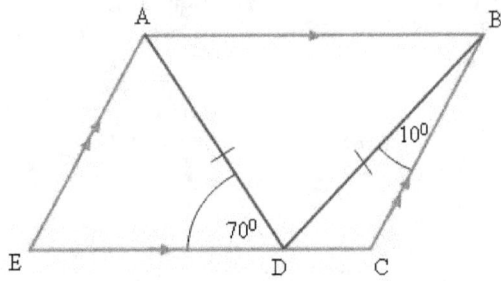

Problem 36 Solution 87

This diagram shows the graph of y = cos x for $0^0 \leq x \leq 360^0$.

Find the values of x which satisfy cos x = -0.39 in the range $0^0 \leq x \leq 360^0$.

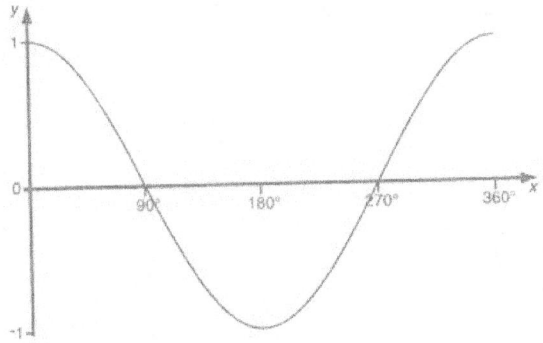

Problem 37 Solution 32

The scale drawing shows a field ABCD.
Tom pitches his tent in the field.
The tent is pitched:

- closer to AB than to AD
- more than 50m from C.

Construct and shade the region where Tom's tent could be pitched.
Leave all your construction lines.

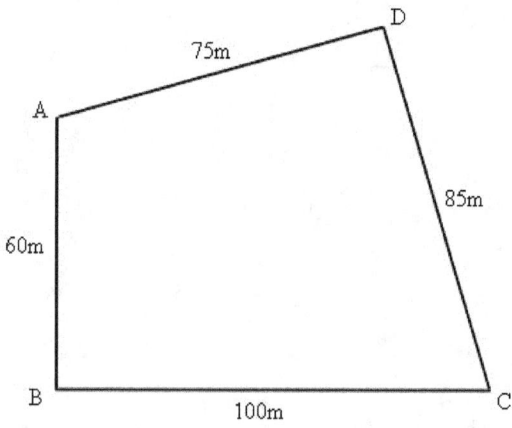

Problem 38 Solution 89

The diagram shows a cyclic quadrilateral, ABCD.
Lines GABH and ECF are parallel.
Angle BCF = 64⁰.

Work out angle ADC.
Give a reason for each angle you work out.

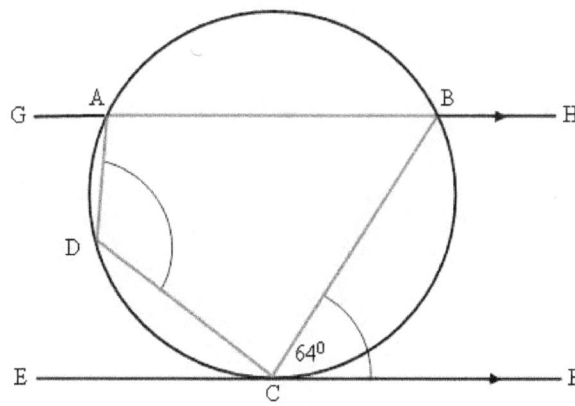

Problem 39 Solution 40

The perimeter of this rectangle is equal to the perimeter of the triangle.

Find the length of the shorter side of the triangle.

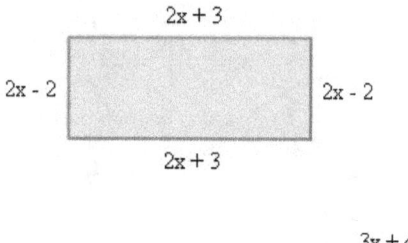

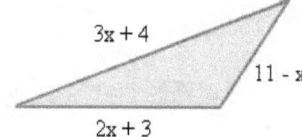

Problem 40 Solution 47

At 09:00 two ships, A and B, leave port P.
  Ship A travels due East.
  Ship B travels on a bearing of 129⁰ at a constant speed.

At 11:30 ship A is 60km from P and due North of ship B, as shown in the diagram.

Work out the speed of ship B.

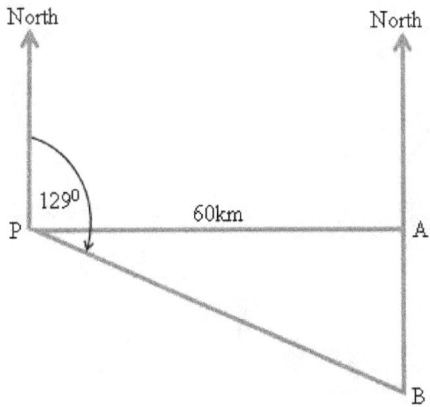

Problem 41 Solution 15

The diagram below shows a trapezium ABCD, with M as the mid-point of AB.

Write the following vectors in terms of p and q.

$\overrightarrow{AD}$ $\overrightarrow{CA}$ $\overrightarrow{DB}$ $\overrightarrow{CM}$ $\overrightarrow{MD}$

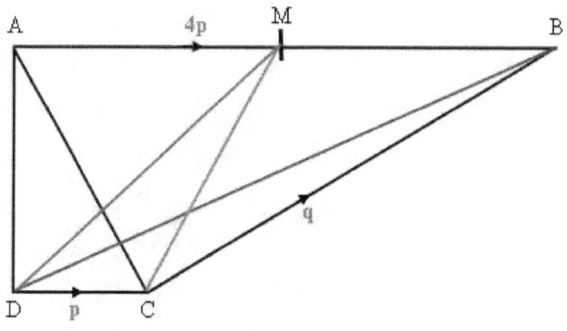

Problem 42 Solution 79

WXYZ is a frustum of a cone.
The base radius, AY, of the frustum is 10m, and the top radius, BZ, is 4m.
VB = 6m, and BA = 9m.

Calculate the volume of the frustum.

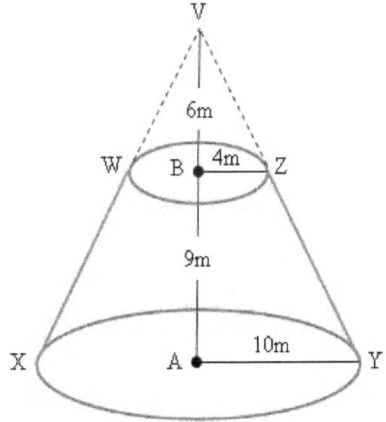

Problem 43 Solution 50

Two lampshades, A and B, are made using the same material.
Lampshade A is the curved surface of a cylinder with radius 14cm
and height 19cm.
Lampshade B is the curved surface of a frustum of a cone.
The frustum is the shape remaining when a cone, radius 15cm, has
a smaller cone radius 5cm, removed from it as shown.

Which lampshade has more material and by how much?

Lampshade A

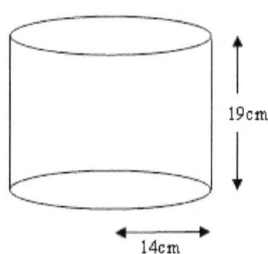

19cm

14cm

Lampshade B

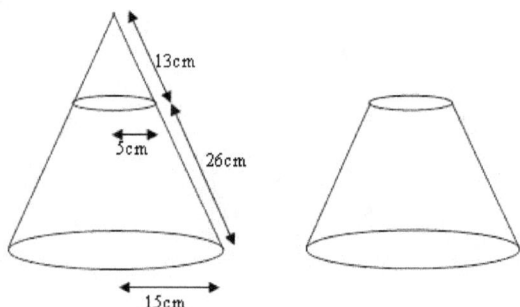

13cm

5cm

26cm

15cm

Problem 44 Solution 31

The diagram shows a park ABCD.
Scale: 1cm represents 100m.

The council wants to put a shed inside the park and it must be;
• nearer to AB than AD
• less than 400m from C.

Shade the region where they can put the shed.
You must show all your construction arcs.

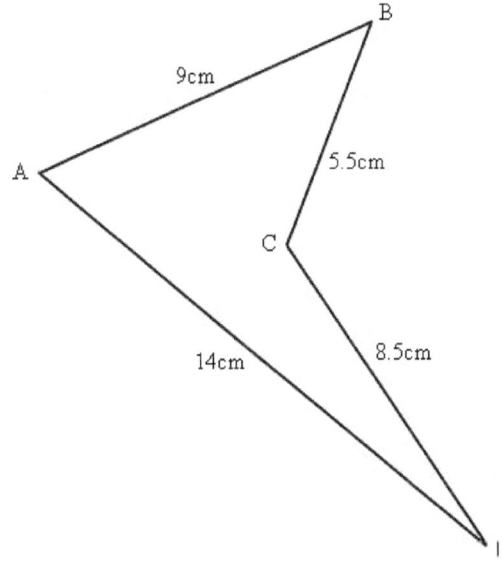

Problem 45 Solution 58

The diagram shows two circles, each of radius 5cm, which touch
at E and have centres at C and F.
AB = 5cm.
ACEF is a straight line.
Line DF is tangent to the circle at D.

Prove that triangles ABE and CDF are congruent.

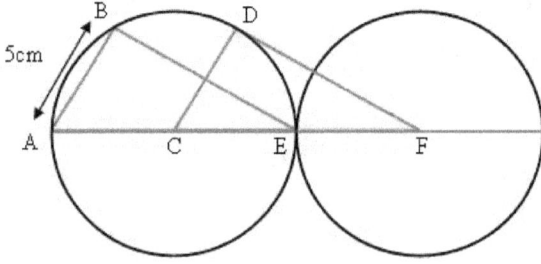

Problem 46 Solution 39

Here is a right-angled triangle.

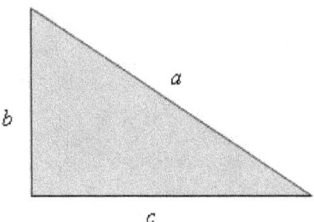

For this triangle:

$$a^2 = b^2 + c^2$$

Calculate the value of c when $a = 2.1 \times 10^5$ cm and $b = 7.6 \times 10^4$ cm. Give your answer in standard form to an appropriate degree of accuracy.

Problem 47 Solution 29

A box is in the shape of a triangular prism.
The cross-section of the prism is an equilateral triangle.
The box is exactly the right size to contain a sphere of radius 5cm.
The sphere touches the five faces of the box.
The diagram below shows a cross-section through the centre of the sphere.

a) Show that the length of a side of the equilateral triangle is
    17.3cm, correct to one decimal place.
a) Calculate the volume of the box.

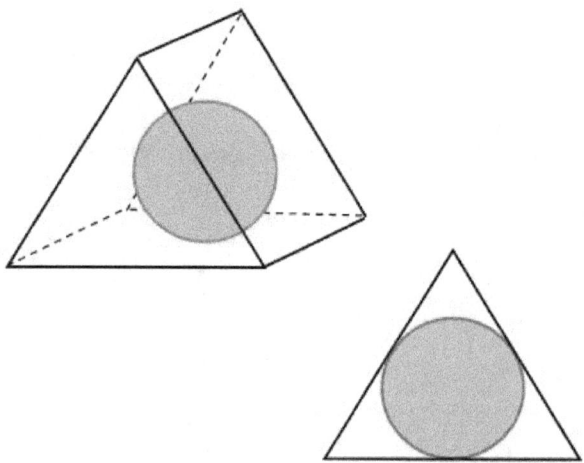

Problem 48 Solution 10

Josh decides he will install an LPG tank in his car's spare wheel space.
Here is a sketch of the tank. It is in the form of a torus.
R is the radius centred on the top of the tank.
r is the radius of a cross-section of the tank.

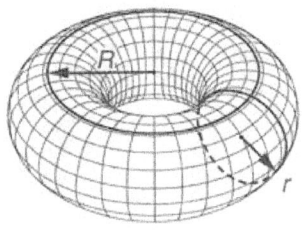

a) The volume, V, of the tank is given by this formula:

$$V = 2 \times \pi^2 \times R \times r^2$$

The largest LPG tank that Josh can fit has $R = 210$mm and $r = 87$mm, each given to the nearest mm.

Work out the minimum volume of this tank, giving your answer correct to 3 significant figures.

b) It is dangerous to fill an LPG tank to more than 80% of its volume.
One litre $= 1 \times 10^6$ mm^3

Work out the greatest number of litres of LPG that Josh should put in this tank.

73

Problem 49 Solution 05

In the diagram ADE is a triangle.
BC is parallel to DE and DBA is parallel to EF.

Work out angle x.
Give reasons for each step of your working.

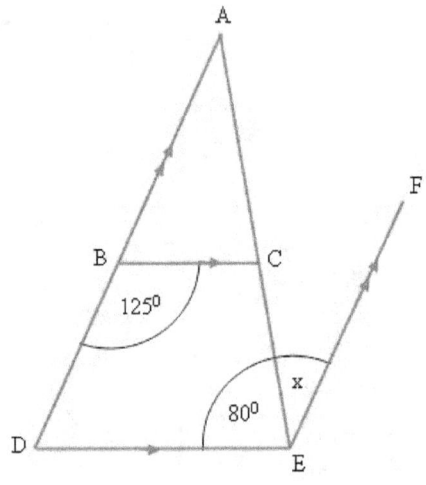

Problem 50 Solution 19

A floor is tiles using a pattern of two different shaped tiles.
One of the shapes is a square and the other is a regular polygon.
At each vertex in the pattern, two of the polygon tiles and one
square tile meet.

What shape is the regular polygon?
Show your reasoning clearly.

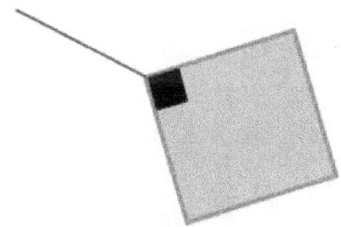

Problem 51 Solution 101

In the sketch below, A is the point (-6, 1) and B is point (3, 4).

a) Write down the coordinates of the midpoint of AB.
b) Write down the vector $\overrightarrow{AB}$.
c) Work out the length of AB.

Write your answer as a surd in the simplest form.

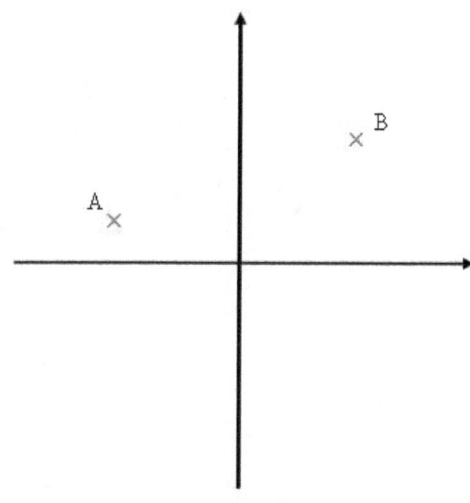

Problem 52 Solution 41

In the diagram, AD is parallel to BC.
Angle ABC = 80⁰, angle CAD = 30⁰ and angle ADC = 70⁰.

Show that triangles ABC and DCA are similar.

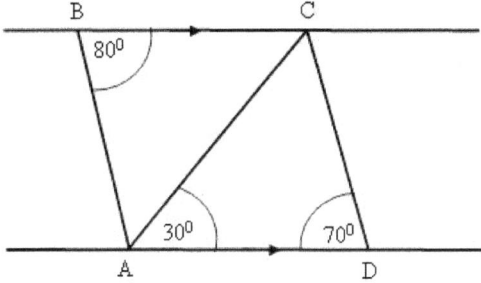

Problem 53 Solution 75

Here is a cone.

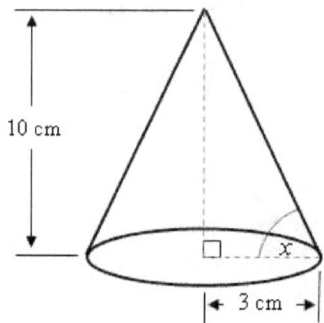

10 cm

3 cm

a) Work out the volume of the cone.
b) Work out angle x, the angle between the slant height and the base.

Problem 54 Solution 06

Three towns, Alet (A), Binley (B) and Swin (S), are shown in the
  diagram below.
The distance between the towns on a map are shown in the
  diagram on the left.
The real distance between Alet and Swin is shown in the diagram
  on the right.
The two triangles are similar.

a) Work out the actual distance between Binley and Swin.
b) Bella walks the 30km between Binley and Swin at an average
    speed of 4km/hour.

Work out the time taken for her to complete her walk.

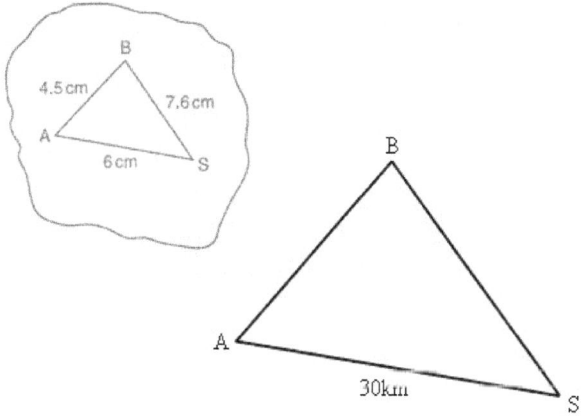

Problem 55 Solution 81

In a biscuit factory, round biscuits 7cm in diameter are cut from a long strip of dough.

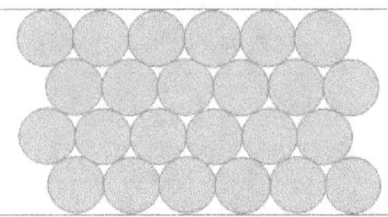

The diagram above shows how may biscuits fit across the strip of dough. To reduce waste, they decide to change to regular hexagonal biscuits. The following diagram shows how many biscuits fit across the strip of dough. The strip of dough is the same width. The manufacturer of the biscuit cutter need to know the length of each side of the hexagonal biscuits.

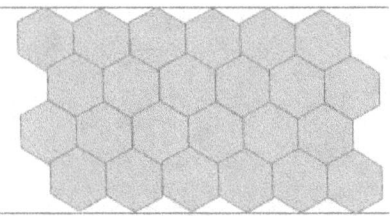

How long is each side of the hexagonal biscuits?

Problem 56 Solution 91

The diagram shows a swimming pool course set out on a lake.
Angle BCA = 90⁰.

Swimmers go from A to B to C and then directly back to A.

a) Calculate the total length of the swimming course.
b) C is due north of A.
   Calculate the bearing of B from A.

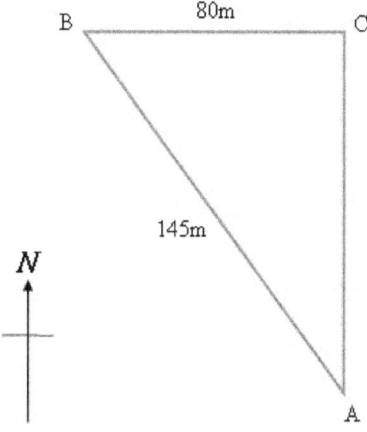

Problem 57 Solution 14

Three of these rectangles are joined together to form two different rectangles.

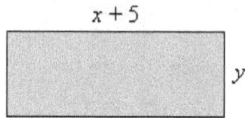

$$x + 5$$

$$y$$

Find an expression for the perimeter of each possible rectangle. Give your answer in the form $ax + by + c$.

Problem 58 Solution 25

Triangle PRS is a right angled triangle
ST is 10 units
TP is x units
RS is 12 units
QT is 4 units
QT is parallel to RS

a) Find the area of QRST
b) B) Find the length of x.

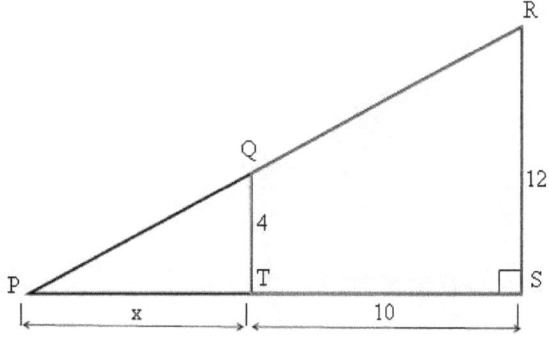

Problem 59 Solution 78

This diagram shows a shape made from two squares and two triangles.
The area of the smaller square is 5cm² and the area of the larger square is 15cm².
Work out the area of the complete shape.
Give your answer in the form $a + b \sqrt{c}$ where c is as small as possible.

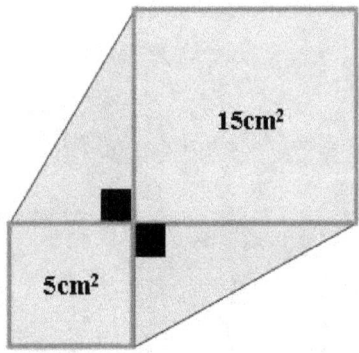

Problem 60 Solution 35

A ship heading due north at a logged speed of 14 knots sights at
position A a lighthouse L at bearing 020° and, at the same time, a known
shipwreck W at bearing 045°, 30 minutes later, the lighthouse is due east
of the ship's new position B and the shipwreck is at bearing 068°.

Find the distance LW between the lighthouse and the shipwreck.

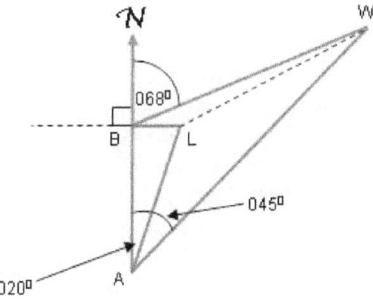

Problem 61 Solution 38

In the diagram below, AB is parallel to CD.

Complete the sentence:

Angle a = ………… because …………………………………………

……………………………………………………………………………

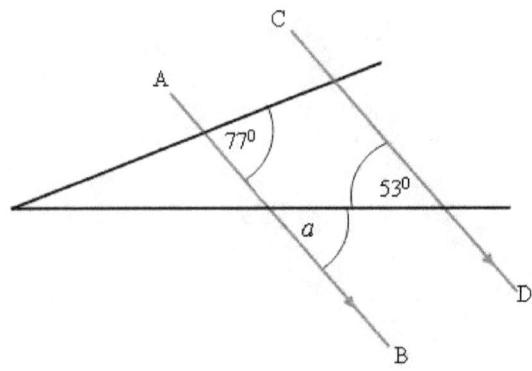

Problem 62 Solution 03

A cheese is a cylinder of radius 7cm and depth 5cm.
The cheese is totally covered with a thin coating of wax.
A slice of the cheese is cut so that the top is the sector of a circle of angle 34⁰.

Work out the area of the wax coating on this slice of cheese.

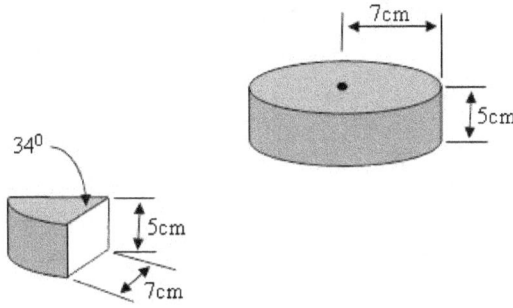

Problem 63 Solution 102

ABC is a triangle.

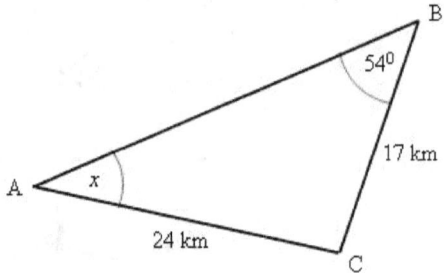

Calculate angle x.

Problem 64 Solution 27

Calculate the size of the two equal angles, each labelled a, in this irregular hexagon.

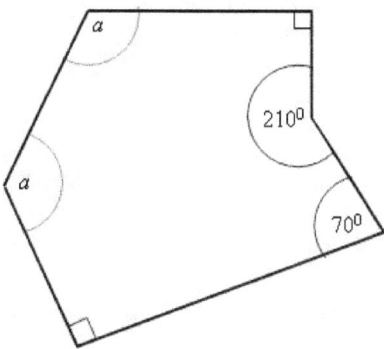

Problem 65 Solution 88

P and Q are towns in different countries.
A water company wants to lay a water pipeline between P and Q.
The company can lay it either in one straight section or in two
straight sections with a connection on the country border.
The cost of laying one kilometre of pipeline in each country is
shown on the diagram below.

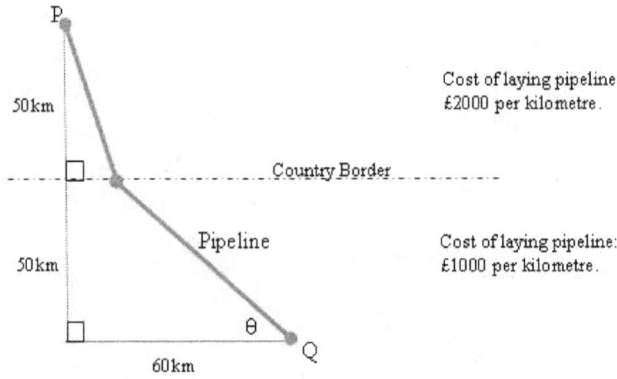

The company has investigated three routes between P and Q.
Work out the costs of these routes.

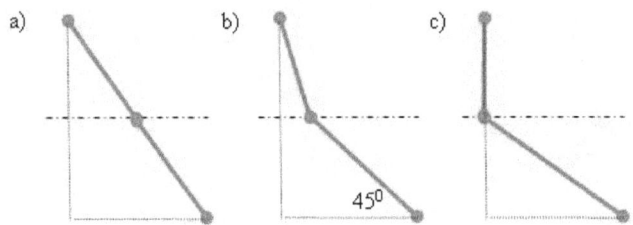

Problem 66 Solution 24

A cuboid is 2cm wide, 3cm high and 6cm long.

Calculate the length of the diagonal PQ.

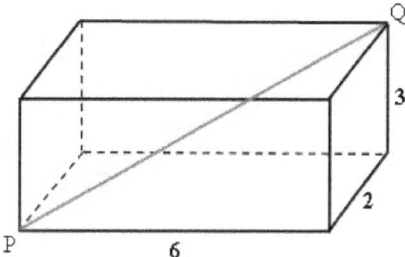

Problem 67 Solution 103

ABCD is a quadrilateral.

The midpoints of AB, BC, CD and DA are P, Q. R and S respectively.

$\overrightarrow{AB}$ = 2e, $\overrightarrow{BC}$ = 2f and $\overrightarrow{CD}$ = 2g.

By first finding the vector AD in terms of e, f and g, prove that PQRS is a parallelogram.

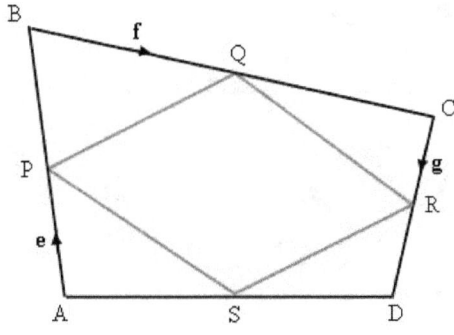

Problem 68 Solution 07

OAB is a sector of circle.

Angle AOB = 80⁰

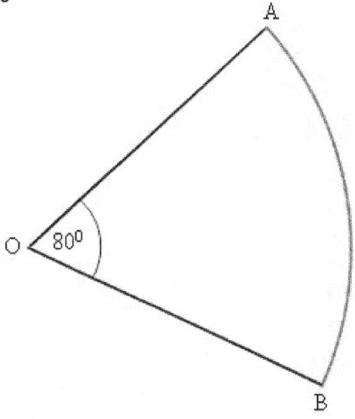

The length of arc AB is 12π cm.

Find the perimeter of the sector, giving your answer in the form $a + b\pi$.

Problem 69a Solution 49

Leigh plays rugby and is about to kick the ball towards the goal.

a) He is standing at L.
    L is 48m from the centre of the goal and 42m from the line TW.
    The distance TC is 35m.

    Calculate LS, the shortest distance from Leigh to the line ST.
    Calculate the angle TCL.

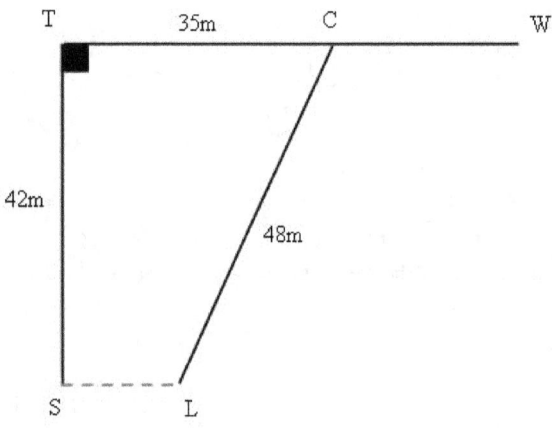

Problem 69b Solution 49

b) Later in the game, Leigh has another kick towards the goal. This time, he ie standing 31m from the line TW and the angle XLC is 25⁰.

Calculate the distance d between Leigh and the centre of the goal.

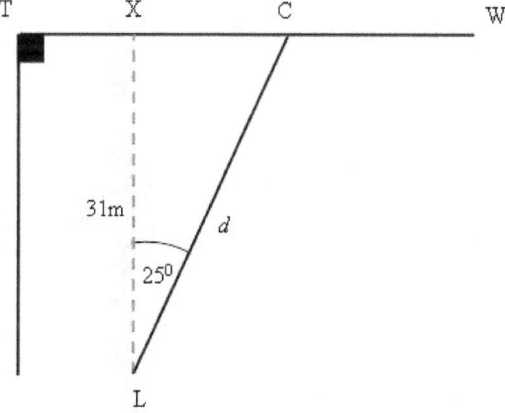

Problem 70 Solution 54

This diagram shows the metal framework on a window.
AB and CD are arcs of circles, each with centre O.

a) Show that the length of arc AB, in cm, is 4π.
b) Work out the total length of metal in the framework.
   Give your answer in the simplest form in terms of π.

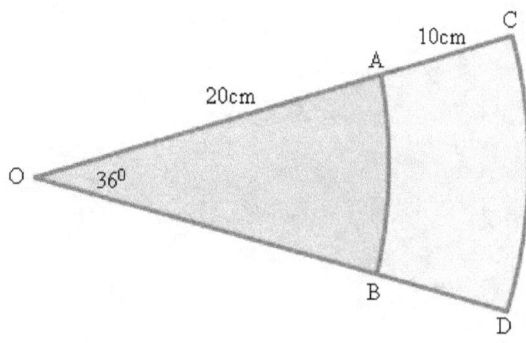

Problem 71 Solution 01

A rectangle is x cm long. Its width is 4 cm shorter than the length. The area of the rectangle is 15 cm².

Work out the value of x. Give your answer correct to two decimal places.

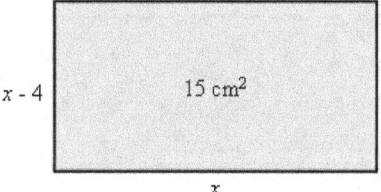

Problem 72 Solution 34

A water container measuring 7 x 18 x 16cm is filled with water up to a height of 6cm.
Four solid steel balls, each with a with a diameter of 5cm, are immersed into the water.

How high will the water rise?
Does the water overflow?

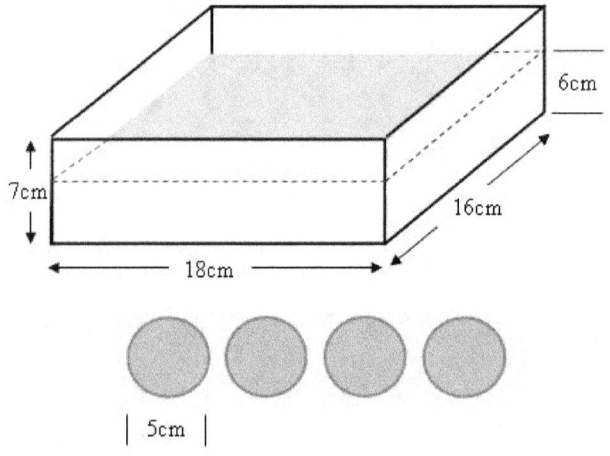

Problem 73 Solution 94

At an awards ceremony, both the first prize and the second prize
are statues.
The statues are mathematically similar and made from the same
material.
The first prize statue is 20cm tall and the second prize statue is
15cm tall.

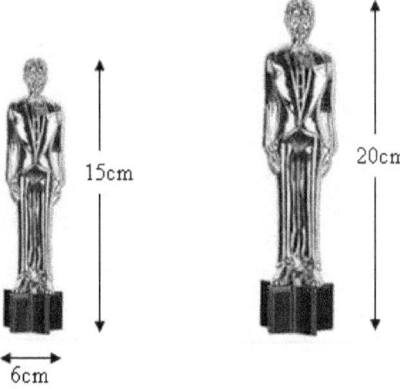

a) The diameter of the base of the smaller statue is 6cm.
    Calculate the diameter of the base of the larger statue.

b) The larger statue has a mass of 700g.
    Calculate the mass of the smaller statue.

Problem 74 Solution 84

Here are two triangles:

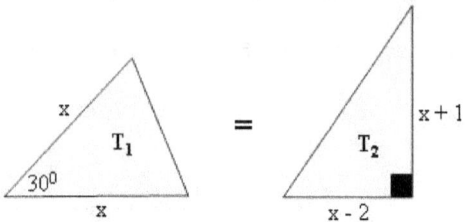

The lengths of the sides are in centimetres.

The area of triangle T_1 is equal to the area of triangle T_2.

Work out the value of x, giving your answer in the form $a \pm \sqrt{b}$ where a and b are integers.

Problem 75 Solution 71

a) Elaine has this triangular piece of material.

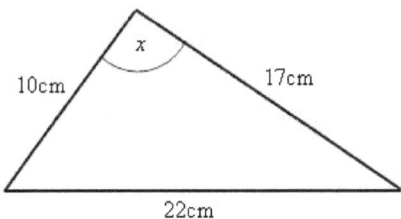

Show that $x = 106^0$ correct to the nearest degree.

b) From the material, Elaine cuts out a sector of a circle, radius 6cm.

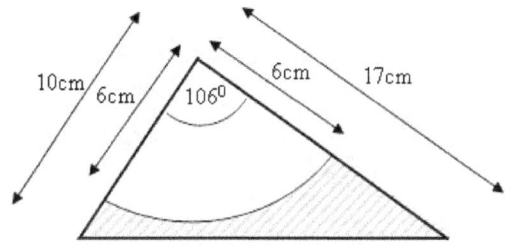

Find the area of the material left over, shown shaded.

Problem 76 Solution 52

The diagram below shows two regular hexagons.
O is the centre of each hexagon.
The larger hexagon is an enlargement of the smaller hexagon,
scale factor 2, centre O.
The midpoints of corresponding sides of these two hexagons are
joined.

What fraction of the larger hexagon is shaded?

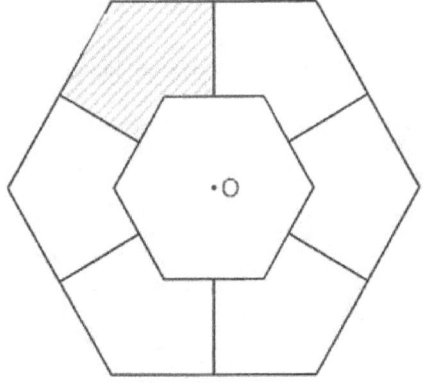

Problem 77 Solution 17

The cube ABCDPQRS has sides 4cm long.
It is drawn on 3D axes where each axis uses a one-centimetre scale.
AB is parallel to the x-axis,
BC is parallel to the y-axis.
CR is parallel to the z-axis.
Point A has coordinates (¯2, ¯1, 0)

Work out the coordinates of the points P, B and R.

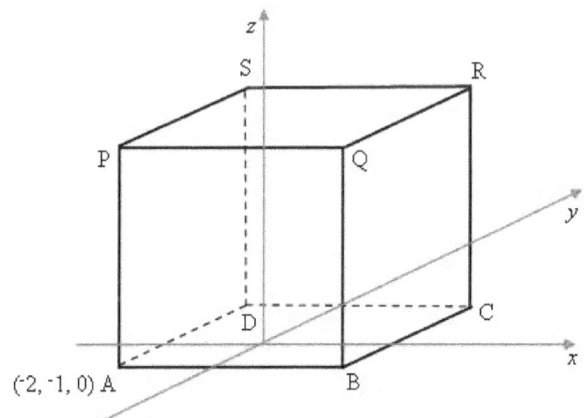

Problem 78 Solution 57

ABCD is a quadrilateral with a right angle at D.
Angle ABC = 110^0, angle BAC = 37^0, angle DAC = 32^0 and
AD = 8.2cm.

a) Show that AC = 9.7cm correct to 1 decimal place.
b) Calculate BC.

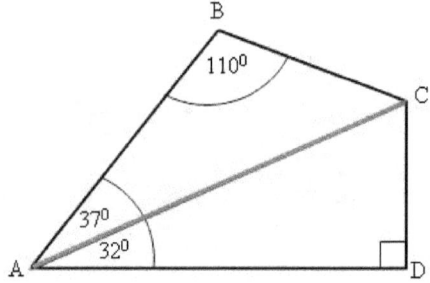

Problem 79 Solution 83

The Jones family decides to buy a new TV.
This sketch shows their old TV.
The screen size of a TV is given as the length of its diagonal.

They decide to buy a new widescreen TV with the same screen
height as their old one.
The diagonal of the new TV is 42 inches, as shown in this sketch.

The screens of these TVs are rectangular.

Calculate how much wider, in inches, the screen on their new TV
is than the screen on their old TV.

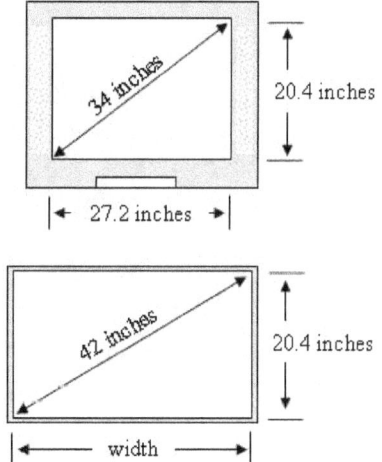

Problem 80 Solution 46

The diagram shows a company logo.
It is a square inside a circle of diameter 6cm.
The vertices of the square lie on the circumference of the circle.

a) Show that the square has sides of length 4.24cm, correct to 2
   decimal places.

b) Work out the percentage of the logo that is shaded.

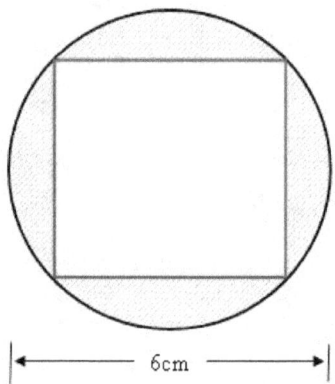

6cm

Problem 81 Solution 56

The sector below is the net for the curved surface of the cone.
All lengths are in centimetres.

a) Calculate h, the height of the cone.
   Give your answer in exact form.
b) A mathematically similar sector has a radius 8cm.
   Find the height of the cone that can be made from this sector.

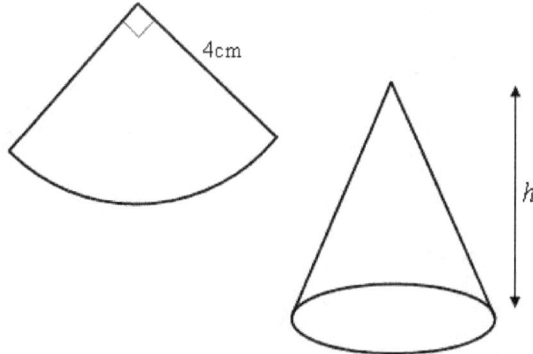

4cm

h

Problem 82 Solution 36

ABCD is a cyclic quadrilateral.
Triangle ABC is isosceles.
XY is a tangent to the circle at D.
Angle ABC = 96^0.
Angle XDA= 54^0.

Prove that AD is parallel to BC.
Give reasons for any angles you calculate.

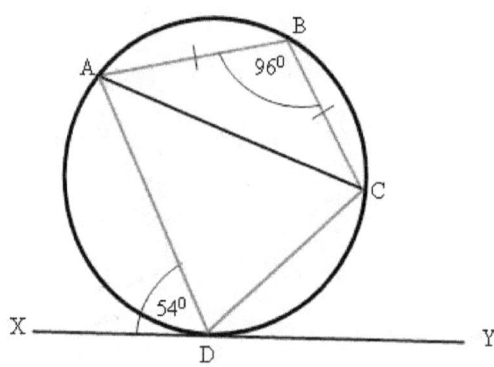

Problem 83 Solution 95

This diagram shows a swimming pool in the shape of a prism.
The swimming pool is empty.
The swimming pool is filled with water at a constant rate of 50 litres per minute.

Work out how long it will take for the swimming pool to be completely full of water.

Give your answer in hours.

(1 m³ = 1000 litres)

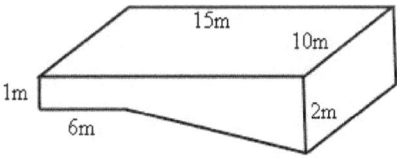

Problem 84 Solution 99

The diagram shows the graph of $y = \sin x$ for $0^0 \le x \le 360^0$

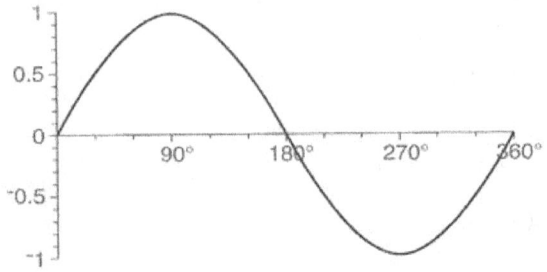

One solution to the equation $\sin x = 0.8$ is $x = 53^0$, correct to the nearest degree.

Find the values of x which satisfy $\sin x = {}^-0.8$ in the range $0^0 \le x \le 360^0$

Problem 85 Solution 105

A pyramid is made in the shape of a square based pyramid.
A box for the paperweight is made from card and is the same
    shape as the paperweight.
A net for the box is drawn on a rectangle of card.

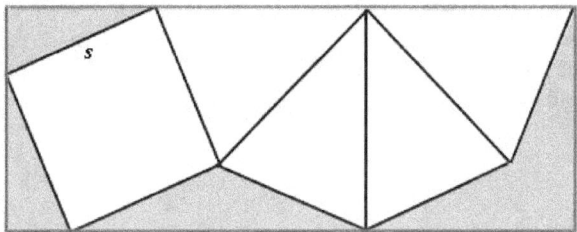

a)   One side of the net is marked s.

    Which side will join to side s when the box is made?

    The box has base length 6.8mm
    The length of each slant edge of the box is 8.9mm
    The top of the pyramid is above the centre of the square base.

b) Show that the angle, a, at the bottom of each triangular face is
    67.5^0.

Problem 86 Solution 65

The diagram shows the journey of a boat starting from A.
To avoid rocks, the boat first travels 5km on a bearing of 068°
to B.
It then travels from B to C.
C is 12km due east of A.

a) Show by calculation that AD, the distance that B is east of A, is
   4.24km correct to 2 decimal places.
b) Calculate the bearing on which the boat travels from B to C.

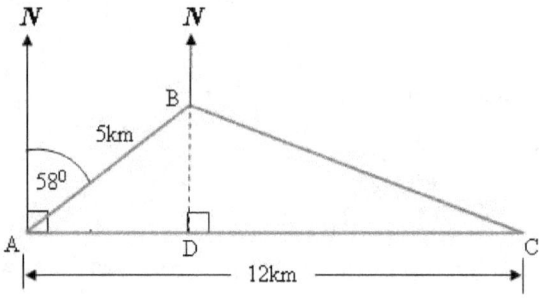

Problem 87 Solution 09

ABC is a triangle.
D is a point on AC.
Angle BAD = 45⁰
Angle ADB = 80⁰
AB = 7.4cm
DC = 5.8cm

Work out the length of BC.

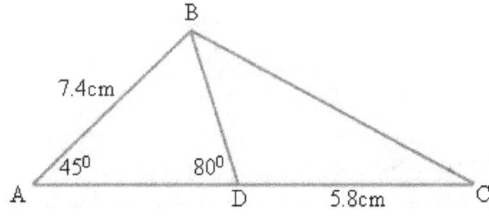

Problem 88 Solution 33

a) Darnby Council uses this litter bin in parks.
   It is a cuboid.

   Calculate the volume of the bin.
   Write your answer in litres.

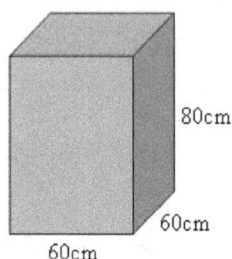

80cm

60cm

60cm

b) Hemby Council's bins have a volume of 120 litres.
   They change to a bin with all the dimensions <u>double</u> those of
   their original bin.

   Calculate the volume of the larger bin.

c) Fairmead Council used a bin with width 45cm, depth 55cm
   and height 60cm.
   They want a new bin which is mathematically similar and has
   <u>three</u> times the volume.

   Calculate the height of the new bin.

Problem 89 Solution 23

A cricket ball is a sphere of radius 3.6cm.

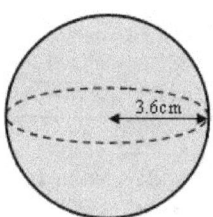

a) Work out the volume of the cricket ball.
b) The mass of the cricket ball is 100g.
   Work out the density of the cricket ball, giving the units in your answer.

Problem 90 Solution 60

This information is given on a pack of rolls of toilet paper:

> 241 sheets per roll
> sheet size 124mm x 104mm
> roll length 29.88m
> total area in the pack 49.72m²

a) Show that the pack contains 16 rolls of paper.
b) The 16 rolls are packaged in an array 4 x 4 x 1.
   The pack has dimensions 464mm x 416mm x 116mm.

   (i) Show that the height of one toilet roll is 104mm and its
       radius is 58mm.

   (ii) The toilet roll cardboard inner has diameter 48mm.
        Work out the thickness of each sheet.

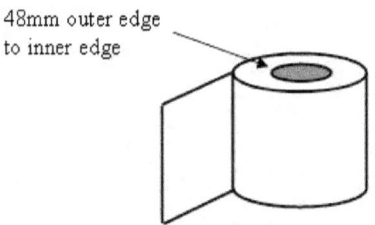

48mm outer edge
to inner edge

Problem 91 Solution 12

A staircase consists of treads of length T and risers of length R, as shown.

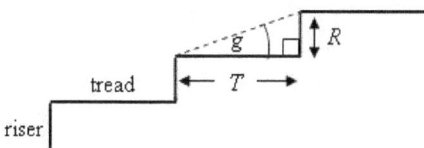

There are four safety requirements:

- T must be at least 220mm
- R must be at most 220mm
- $T + 2R$ must be at least 550mm and at most 700mm
- Angle g must not be more than 42^0

Russell wants a staircase with T = 222mm and R = 218mm
These values satisfy the first two safety requirements.

Show whether these values satisfy each of the other two safety requirements.

Problem 92 Solution 55

Here is a diagram of a Park, ABCD.

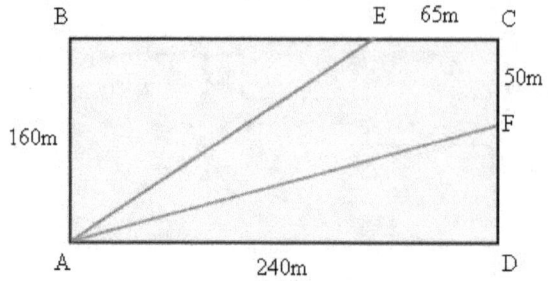

E is a point on BC and F is a point on CD.
EC = 65m and CF = 50m.

The perimeter of the park is a rectangle measuring 160m by 240m.
There are straight paths around the perimeter of the park and from A to E, and A to F.

Mary has to use the paths.

Calculate the shortest distance she has to walk to get from A to C.

Problem 93 Solution 43

A(0,2), B(7,9), and C(6,10) are points on the circumference of a circle.

a) Find the length of AC.
b) Prove that the triangle ABC has a right-angle at B.
c) Show that the centre of the circle is (3,6) and has a radius of 5.
d) Find the equation of the circle.

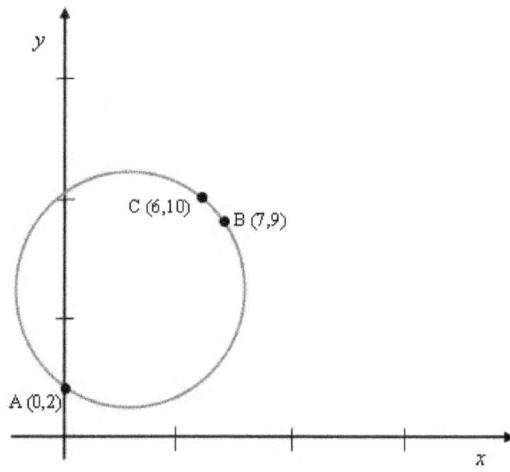

Problem 94 Solution 74

Triangle ABC is right-angled at C such that tan B = 2.

Calculate the possible lengths of all the sides of the triangle.

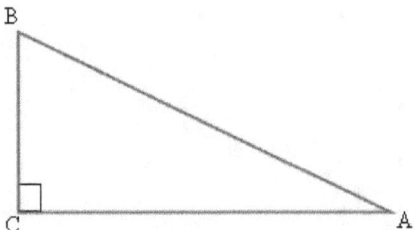

Problem 95 Solution 73

A box is a cuboid measuring 3cm by 7cm by 8cm.
A stick of length 10cm is placed n the box with one end of the stick
in one corner of the box, as shown in the diagram.

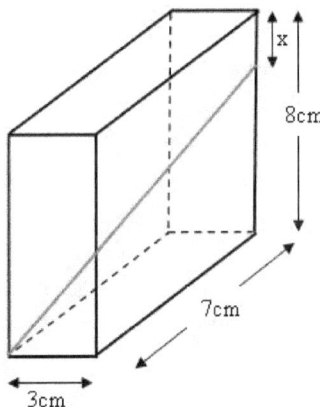

a) Show that x, the distance of the upper end of the stick from
   the top corner of the box, is 1.5cm correct to one decimal
   place.

b) Work out the angle that the stick makes with the base of the
    box.

Problem 96 Solution 98

AB is a side of a square.
A is the point with coordinates (4,3), B is the point with
coordinates (10,6).

Calculate the area of the square.

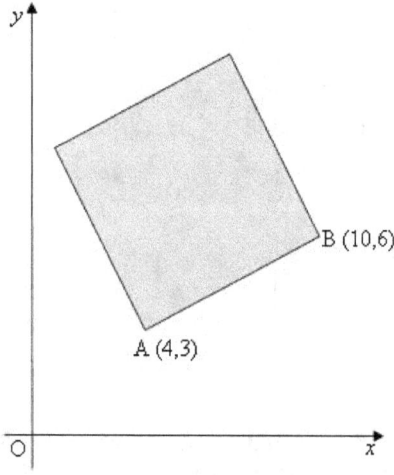

Problem 97 Solution 22

The shape below is made of two semicircles and a straight line.
AB = 10cm. C is the midpoint of AB.

Calculate the perimeter of the shape.

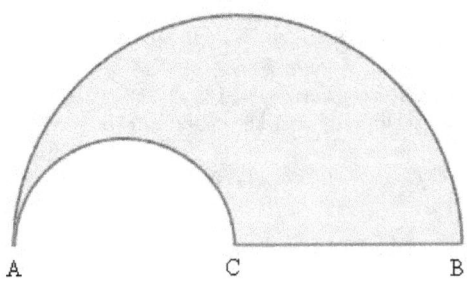

A   C   B

Problem 98 Solution 08

Terry applies for funding to set up a community skate park.
He writes a letter of application.

The probability of being successful is 1/10.

If his letter is unsuccessful, he can appeal. The probability of
success at the appeal is 1/3.

a) Complete the tree diagram.
b) Work out the probability that he is successful in getting funding.

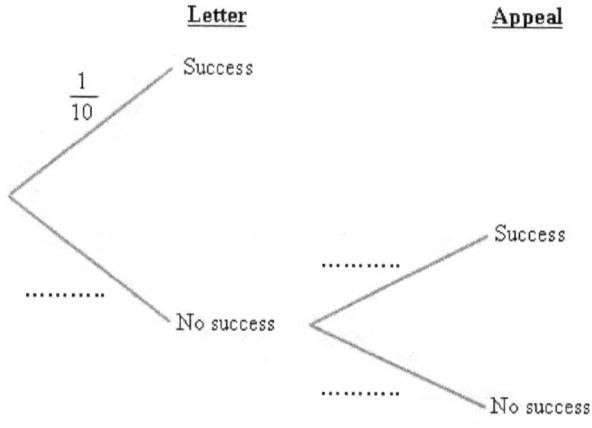

Problem 99 Solution 44

In the diagram, ADE is a triangle.
BC is parallel to DE and DBA is parallel to EF.

Work out angle x.

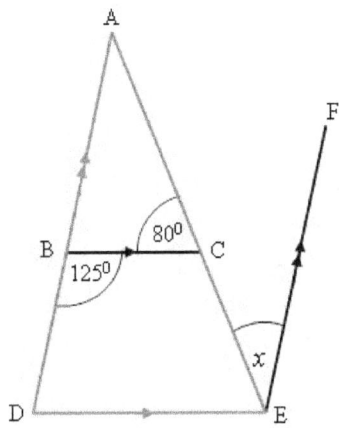

Problem 100 Solution 93

A solid metal cylinder of radius 5cm and length 18cm is melted down and made into spheres of radius 2cm.

Assuming that none of the metal is lost in the process, work out how many of the spheres can be made.

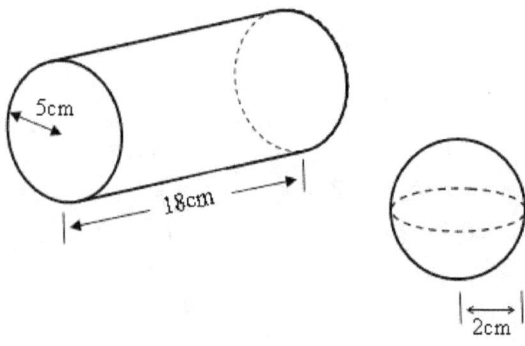

Problem 101 Solution 86

OACB is a parallelogram.

$\overrightarrow{OA}$ = a, and $\overrightarrow{OB}$ = b
D is the point such that $\overrightarrow{AC}$ = $\overrightarrow{CD}$
The point N divides AB in the ratio 2:1.

a) Write an expression for $\overrightarrow{ON}$ in terms of a and b.
b) Prove that OND is a straight line.

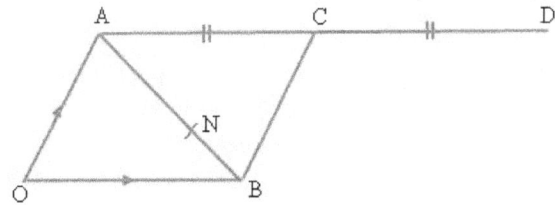

Problem 102 Solution 92

EBC is parallel to AD.
Triangle ABE is isosceles with AE = AB.
Angle BAD is 75⁰.

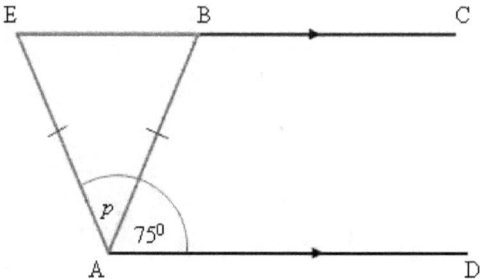

Work out the size of angle *p*.

Problem 103 Solution 90

Here is a triangle.

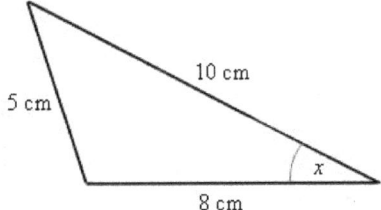

a) Show that $x = 29.7^0$, correct to one decimal place.
b) Work out the area of the triangle.

Problem 104 Solution 76

Josh is tiling a wall.
He needs to cut a tile to the shape shown in the diagram.
Work out angle z.

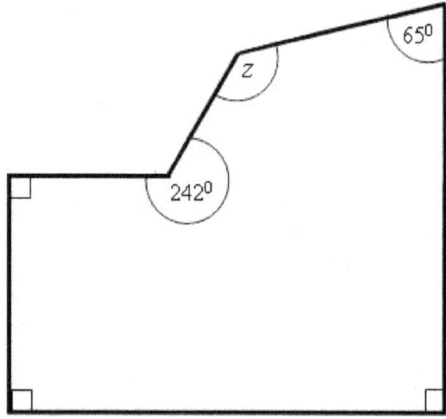

Problem 105 Solution 59

This is a sketch of the graph of $y = x^2$.

One the same axes, sketch the graph of $y = (x + 2)^2$.

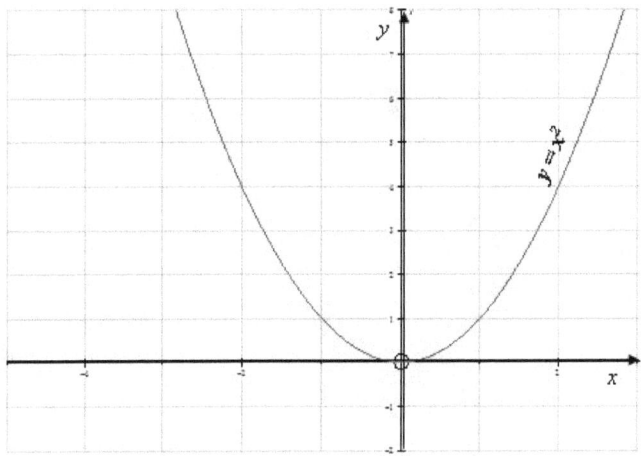

Problem 106 Solution 20

Here is a number pyramid.
The value in each cell is found by adding the values in the two cells beneath it.

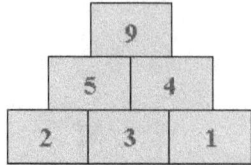

In the number pyramid below, find the value of x.
Show all your workings.

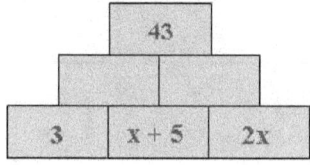

Problem 107 Solution 11

ABCDEFGH is a cuboid.

a) Calculate the length of the diagonal AC.
b) Calculate the length of AG.
c) Calculate angle a

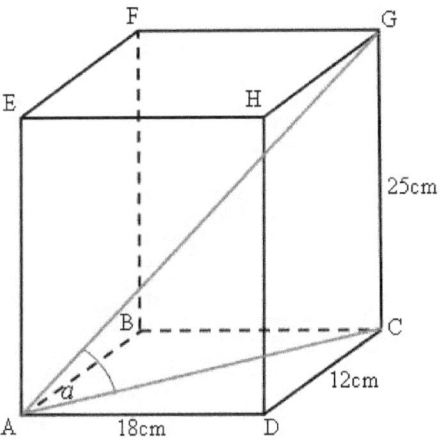

Easy as you Go!

'Easy as you Go' was originally intended to be solely a support for the learning of Mathematics. However it has evolved into something more than just that. The two volumes are packed with a total of 950 pages of mathematics, covering no less than 230 topics and containing a multitude of worked examples, equations and formulas, graphs and charts, tables, diagrams and illustrations.

Together, the two volumes address all the significant issues encountered in First School, Secondary School and in Advanced studies, along with a plethora of anecdotal topics to capture the reader's imagination, and titivate their perhaps otherwise sanguine attitude towards Mathematics.

'Easy as you Go' is ideally suited to student, educator and parent alike because of its simplistic, down-to-earth and visual approach.

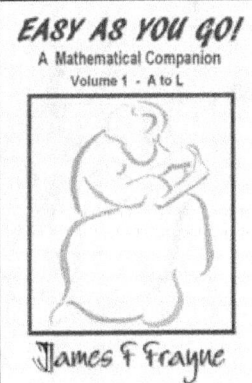

EASY AS YOU GO!
A Mathematical Companion
Volume 1 - A to L

James F Frayne

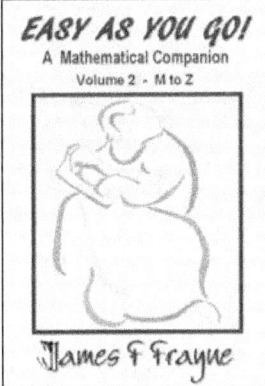

EASY AS YOU GO!
A Mathematical Companion
Volume 2 - M to Z

James F Frayne